Would You Rather Game Book

for Kids and Teens - Tough Edition:

66 Yucky, Gross, Disgusting and Hilarious Questions for the whole Family.

TONI BERRY

Table of Contents

Rules

It is a simple game, which is easy to understand and play, and it will definitely have everyone laughing and talking on any parties.

All you need is a set of gross, wacky, yucky, weird and disgusting questions and at least two players.

- ❖ Choose a player to go first. One player is asked a question at one time. Once he or she has answered the question, the rest of the players answer the same question (optional).
- ❖ There is no winner or loser in the game. It is just a fun twist to a normal truth or dare kind of a game.
- ❖ No player that is asked a "Would you rather" question can answer "both" or "neither." You must choose one of the two options given.
- ❖ Play continues until players are out of questions or for however long you like.
- ❖ Have a tough time!

Would you rather questions

Would you rather drink a gallon of milk within an hour or eat two jars of pickles?

Would you rather have a pig's patch or donkey ears?

Would you rather sweat a lot all the time or pee every 5 minutes?

Would you rather poop out one butter knife or poop 1000 liters of mayonnaise?

Would you rather eat your own pimples or your own scabs?

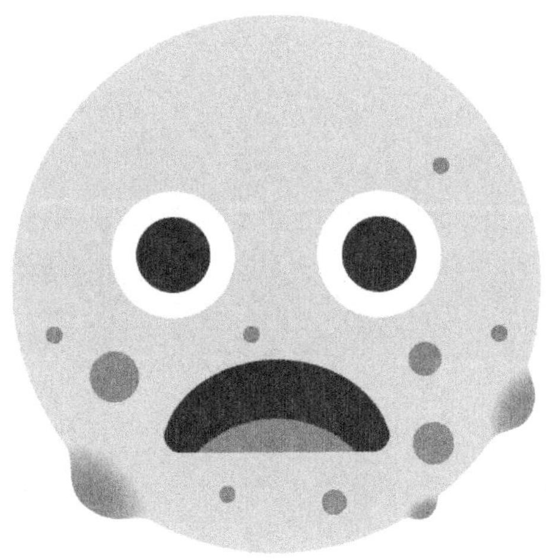

Would you rather wash a corpse or sleep beside one?

Would you rather live in a world full of zombies or a world full of aliens?

Would you rather find yourself in a desert or in a jungle?

Would you rather meet cannibals or tigers in a desert island?

Would you rather chew a piece of gum you found on the floor or a piece of something you don't know what?

Would you rather have lice in your head or no hair at all?

Would you rather have to use a public toilet that is extremely dirty and dark or one that has a snake in it?

Would you rather stay for 5 minutes in a bath with worms or in a swimming pool with crocodile?

Would you rather start burping every time you see your teacher or start farting every time you see your friends?

Would you rather clean 10 public dirty toilets or lick 1 toilet seat in a public toilet?

Would you rather have a hole in your front teeth and be able to smile or have perfect teeth but not be able to smile?

Would you rather have a stomach ache or headache?

Would you rather laugh every time you fart or cry every time your burp?

Would you rather drink a coffee cup full of slugs or eat a hair filled hot dog?

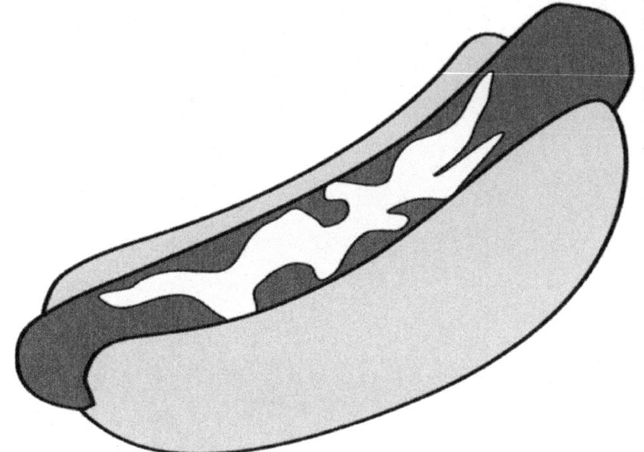

Would you rather be stinky or have pimples all over?

Would you rather have small but painful pimple on your back or big but painless pimple on your face?

Would you rather have a rewind button or a pause button in your life?

Would you rather have clean but only one outfit to wear every day or wear different but dirty clothes every day?

Would you rather have a haircut like your grandparent has or have your grandparent get your haircut done?

Would you rather always smell like a dog or never wear any deodorant?

Would you rather walk like a monkey or talk like a pig?

Would you rather live in uninhabited island for 15 years or be in jail for 5 years?

Would you rather eat peanut butter that smells like poop or tastes like poop?

Would you rather burp confetti or fart with sparkles?

Would you rather never be able to smile or never be able to cry?

Would you rather have an uncontrollable itch in your throat or feet?

Would you rather have a horse bite your back or an elephant bite your back with its trunk?

Would you rather stay in one room with a crocodile or a wolf?

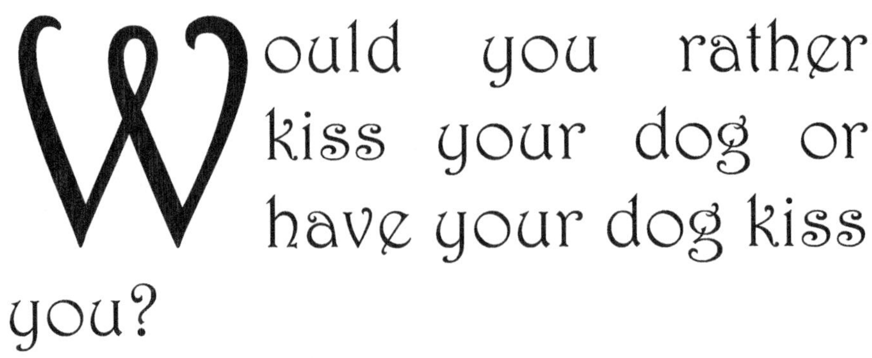 ould you rather kiss your dog or have your dog kiss you?

Would you rather get married to a zombie or a vampire?

Would you rather have no toenails or no fingernails?

Would you rather have your ear or nose be bitten off?

Would you rather burn your fingers or get paper cut?

Would you rather pop a zit on someone's forehead or lick your own zit?

Would you rather never eat pizza again or never eat ice cream again?

Would you rather have to pee every 10 minutes or never have to pee again?

Would you rather have a mouth the size of a pea or have eyes the size of a pea?

Would you rather have eyes on the place of ears or have ears on the place of eyes?

Would you rather eat a hot dog with dandruff or eat diarrhea from a baby?

Would you rather chew a piece of plastic or a piece of rubber?

Would you rather be a bear child or a wolf child?

Would you rather have really bad dandruff or only use dog shampoo?

Would you rather sleep in a very dark room or do not sleep for 3 nights?

Would you rather drink seawater or toilet water?

Would you rather be mute or be able to speak only to animals?

Would you rather become now 4 year old or 40 year old?

Would you rather be bitten by mosquitoes or have a cat scratch your face?

Would you rather wear the same outfit without washing it or go without bathing for a month?

Would you rather wear someone's socks or someone's underwear?

Would you rather poop your pants or use a disgusting toilet?

Would you rather lick pus from someone's pimple or lick someone's eye crust?

Would you rather chew on sand or shell crumb?

Would you rather lick someone's armpit or have someone else lick your armpit?

Would you rather have lice in your head or poop your pants?

Would you rather be live alone on an island or be lost at sea for a month?

Would you rather eat a rotten apple or a sour watermelon?

Would you rather have flu or a chickenpox?

Would you rather poo on someone every day or have someone poop on you once a week?

Would you rather eat a small can of dog food or six overripe bananas?

Would you rather show up to school with no pants for the rest of your life or pee yourself in front of your classmates every time you have a presentation?

Would you rather sneeze every time someone calls your name or feel intense pain every time someone says hello to you?

Have a tough time!

Printed in Great Britain
by Amazon